Little People, BIG DREAMS™
HELEN KELLER

Written by
Maria Isabel Sánchez Vegara

Illustrated by
Sam Rudd

Frances Lincoln
Children's Books

Once, at a farm in northern Alabama, USA, a little baby called Helen was born. From the very beginning, her curious mind was eager to learn. She was just one when she said "water," a word she would never forget.

Helen was only 19 months old when she got a terrible fever that left her deaf and blind. From that day on, she had to get used to living in a dark and silent world. Still, she could smell the sweet scent of flowers and feel her parents' hugs.

By the time that she was six, Helen had created more than 60 signs to communicate with her playmate Martha, like a pull to mean "come" or a nod for "yes." She could even recognize people by the way the floor shook as they walked.

Touching people's lips, she noticed that others used their mouths to talk. Yet, no matter how hard she tried to do the same, nothing ever happened. It was so frustrating that Helen screamed and kicked until she broke down in tears.

Looking desperately for help, her parents contacted the Perkins Institution for the Blind, which sent one of its brightest students. Her name was Anne Sullivan, and she did not just become Helen's teacher, but her lifelong friend.

The day after they met, Anne gave Helen a gift from the children at her school. She slowly spelled the letters of the name of the gift into her hand: "d-o-l-l." Helen repeated it with her fingers, without knowing she was spelling a word, or even what a word was.

It was weeks later when Anne spelled "w-a-t-e-r," that something amazing happened: a memory of that word came back to Helen. She realized that words were related to things, and that everything had a common name!

That discovery changed Helen's life. She was learning to talk with others! Soon she was reading books in braille, a system that uses tiny bumps on paper to spell words, and the following year, she attended a school for blind people.

Later, Helen met a well-known teacher of deaf people, called Sarah Fuller. Resting her fingers on Sarah's lips, nose, and neck, Helen learned how every sound felt, and, before long, she was able to speak, too.

She became the first deafblind person to earn a Bachelor of Arts degree, and the first to write a book about her life.

After graduating from college, she and Anne traveled the country, sharing Helen's story and giving disabled people a voice.

She wrote another 13 books and hundreds of great speeches that every president of the United States wanted to hear. Yet she preferred to enjoy the company of good friends, like the writer Mark Twain and the inventor Alexander Graham Bell.

Many schools for the deaf and the blind were set up thanks to Helen, and she helped to make braille the world's writing system for the blind. Still, she also found time to defend women's votes and the rights of African-American people.

And, while meeting every obstacle in her way, little Helen learned that everything she had been looking for was already within her, because the best things in life are those that we can feel with our hearts.

HELEN KELLER

(Born 1880 – Died 1968)

1887

1904

Helen Adams Keller was raised in Tuscumbia, Alabama, the daughter of a wealthy family. Although she could both hear and see from birth, she contracted an illness that left her deaf and blind at 19 months old. During her early years, Helen had limited ways of communicating with the world but developed hand-signs with her playmate, Martha, the family cook's daughter. At the age of six, she met Anne Sullivan, a teacher who became her lifelong friend. Helen learned how to finger-spell, beginning with the word "doll." At first, she struggled and found it frustrating, but after lots of practice, Helen mastered the alphabet. She learned how to lip-read by placing her fingers on the lips and throat of the speaker to feel the vibrations that were made during speech.

1945   c.1950s

Helen earned admission to Radcliffe College and graduated with a Bachelor of Arts degree in 1904, the first deafblind person to do so. With Anne's help, Helen wrote her first book, *The Story of My Life*, which has been translated into 50 languages and is still available to read today. Alongside her writing, Helen tackled social and political issues and participated in many campaigns and enterprises to raise money and support for disabled people. After Anne's death, Helen worked with other companions on her mission. She traveled across the world, visiting 35 countries on five continents and meeting many word leaders. Helen Keller remains one of history's greatest campaigners: a person who devoted her life to making the world a better place for everyone.

Want to find out more about **Helen Keller?**

Have a read of these great books:

DK Life Stories: Helen Keller by Libby Romero and Charlotte Ager

The Story of Helen Keller by Christine Platt

Brimming with creative inspiration, how-to projects, and useful information to enrich your everyday life, quarto.com is a favorite destination for those pursuing their interests and passions.

Text © 2022 Maria Isabel Sánchez Vegara. Illustrations © 2022 Sam Rudd.

Little People Big Dreams and Pequeña&Grande are registered trademarks of Alba Editorial, SLU for books, publications and e-books. Produced under licence from Alba Editorial, SLU.

First Published in the USA in 2022 by Frances Lincoln Children's Books, an imprint of The Quarto Group.
Quarto Boston North Shore, 100 Cummings Center, Suite 265D, Beverly, MA 01915, USA
Tel: +1 978-282-9590, Fax: +1 978-283-2742 www.Quarto.com

All rights reserved.

No part of this publication may be reproduced, stored in a retrieval system, or transmitted, in any form, or by any means, electrical, mechanical, photocopying, recording or otherwise without the prior written permission of the publisher or a licence permitting restricted copying.

This book is not authorised, licenced, or approved by the estate of Helen Keller.
Any faults are the publisher's who will be happy to rectify for future printings.
A catalogue record for this book is available from the Library of Congress.
ISBN 978-0-7112-5954-6
Set in Futura BT.

Published by Peter Marley • Designed by Sasha Moxon
Edited by Lucy Menzies and Claire Saunders • Production by Nikki Ingram
Editorial Assistance from Rachel Robinson
Manufactured in Guangdong, China CC062022
1 3 5 7 9 8 6 4 2

Photographic acknowledgements (pages 28-29, from left to right): 1. Helen Keller Holding Pet Poodle in Chair © Bettmann via Getty Images. 2. Helen Keller (1880-1968). /n American writer and lecturer. Photographed at the time of her graduation from Radcliffe College in 1904 © Granger Historical Picture Archive via Alamy Images. 3. Helen Keller was left blind, deaf, and mute by illness when 19 months old. She was educated by Anne Sullivan, and became a lecturer on behalf of the blind. She authored several books. © Oscar White/Corbis/VCG via Getty Images. 4. Helen Keller, c. 1950s © Everett Collection Historical via Alamy Images

Collect the Little People, BIG DREAMS™ series:

FRIDA KAHLO	COCO CHANEL	MAYA ANGELOU	AMELIA EARHART	AGATHA CHRISTIE	MARIE CURIE	ROSA PARKS	AUDREY HEPBURN

EMMELINE PANKHURST	ELLA FITZGERALD	ADA LOVELACE	JANE AUSTEN	GEORGIA O'KEEFFE	HARRIET TUBMAN	ANNE FRANK	MOTHER TERESA

JOSEPHINE BAKER	L. M. MONTGOMERY	JANE GOODALL	SIMONE DE BEAUVOIR	MUHAMMAD ALI	STEPHEN HAWKING	MARIA MONTESSORI	VIVIENNE WESTWOOD

MAHATMA GANDHI	DAVID BOWIE	WILMA RUDOLPH	DOLLY PARTON	BRUCE LEE	RUDOLF NUREYEV	ZAHA HADID	MARY SHELLEY

MARTIN LUTHER KING JR.	DAVID ATTENBOROUGH	ASTRID LINDGREN	EVONNE GOOLAGONG	BOB DYLAN	ALAN TURING	BILLIE JEAN KING	GRETA THUNBERG

JESSE OWENS	JEAN-MICHEL BASQUIAT	ARETHA FRANKLIN	CORAZON AQUINO	PELÉ	ERNEST SHACKLETON	STEVE JOBS	AYRTON SENNA

LOUISE BOURGEOIS	ELTON JOHN	JOHN LENNON	PRINCE	CHARLES DARWIN	CAPTAIN TOM MOORE	HANS CHRISTIAN ANDERSEN	STEVIE WONDER

MEGAN RAPINOE	MARY ANNING	MALALA YOUSAFZAI	ANDY WARHOL	RUPAUL	MICHELLE OBAMA	MINDY KALING	IRIS APFEL

ROSALIND FRANKLIN	RUTH BADER GINSBURG	MARILYN MONROE	KAMALA HARRIS	ALBERT EINSTEIN	CHARLES DICKENS	YOKO ONO	MICHAEL JORDAN

NELSON MANDELA	PABLO PICASSO	AMANDA GORMAN	GLORIA STEINEM	FLORENCE NIGHTINGALE	HARRY HOUDINI	J.R.R. TOLKIEN	ELVIS PRESLEY

NEIL ARMSTRONG	ALEXANDER VON HUMBOLDT	NIKOLA TESLA	WILMA MANKILLER	MARCUS RASHFORD	LAVERNE COX	MAE JEMISON	DWAYNE JOHNSON

HELEN KELLER

ACTIVITY BOOKS

STICKER ACTIVITY BOOK

COLORING BOOK

LITTLE ME, BIG DREAMS JOURNAL

Discover more about the series at www.littlepeoplebigdreams.com